Power from the "P": Phenomenal Poets

Power from the "P": Phenomenal Poets

Phillips High Schools Young Phenomenal Poets

An Anthology of Student Work from Wendell Phillips High School
Chicago, Illinois

School Success Press
San Jose New York Lincoln Shanghai

Power from the "P": Phenomenal Poets

School Success Press
an imprint of iUniverse, Inc.

For information address:
iUniverse, Inc.
5220 S. 16th St., Suite 200
Lincoln, NE 68512
www.iuniverse.com

ISBN: 0-595-21571-8

Printed in the United States of America

The Who and the How

This student anthology seemed to spring from our students' abilities as well as their over-bounding potential and our determination to show what a group of forgotten kids can do. It has been a pleasure to work with the talented individuals who authored this book. We set the bar of expectations high and they soared beyond them. They constantly amaze us.

After all of our efforts, we have compiled the 1st collection of our young and truly "Phenomenal Poets" work. Our ideas and their work have been realized thanks to the sponsorship of the Michael Jordan Foundation.

We would like to thank the students for their hard work, eagerness and for teaching two teachers a thing or two about life.

Thank you and enjoy!

Molly Dunlea and Martina Brockway

Student Dedications

Earl Norman:
This book is dedicated to God for his ray of light.
To my mother and father for giving me life.
To the teens inspired by nothing.
To the adults with garbage but made it into something.
To the teachers that treated me as if I was their son.
Last but not least, to my loved ones.

Victoria Holmes:
I like to dedicate my work to all people who feel like life is unexplainable, and can't describe what they feel at that time. Many people say what I write is how they felt. my poetry is my expressions. I dedicate my work to the people who make me feel emotions. My emotions give me a reason to express myself. Thank you for your support.

Christopher Crowder:
This dedication goes to the world
To the hate—for teaching me about evil
To the good—for teaching me about surviving and that there are good people in this world
I thank the emotion and pain I received that helped me express and strengthen my words in my poems
The Lord, for giving me the mind, ideas, and soul to write my poetry
My parents for raising me the best they can
My educators for teaching me how to read and write
My family who's been there and those in heave who knew me
Without the good, evil, God, family, teachers, my mind, the world, and love given to me by loved ones, this wouldn't be possible
I also thank my ancestors for bringing me in the world
Last but not least, the people who read and understand my poems.

Danny Dean:
I would like 2 thank my brother
Who raised me
My niece
Who tamed me
My cousinz 4 teachin me how 2 flow
How much I appreciate that they will never know
My tru dogz who passed away
I goin 2 meet ya'll again 1 day
4 the peoplez like me thatz still strugglin
And all the dogz that still thuggin
Keep ya'll head above the water
Cause there iz gonna be a brighter 2morrow

How to Read a Poem

By Edward Hirsch
Poetry Editor of *Double Take* magazine

Read these poems to yourself in the middle of the night.
Turn on a single lamp and read them while you're alone
in an otherwise dark room
or while someone else sleeps next to you.
Read them when you're wide awake in the early morning, fully alert.
Say them over to yourself in a place where silence reigns and the din of
the culture—the constant buzzing noise that surrounds us—
has momentarily stopped.

Creations of the Cast

Photographs by: Earl Norman and Drawing by: James Cannon

Can you feel my physical expression?
Do my words send your minds on a mission?
Can you understand the poetic words?
Do the lyrics make you think you can't believe what you just heard?
Can you see the pictures I describe through my eyes?
Do I say things that leave you surprised?
Can you stand hearing the truth-I hate telling lies?
Do I put you under a spell, that leaves you hypnotized?
Can you see what I've been through?
Do I remind myself of you?
Can you listen to what I'm saying mentally and physically?
No matter what—just feel me.

By: Earl Norman

I REMEMBER...

Don't you fall now—
For I'se still goin', honey,
I'se still climbin',
And life for me ain't been no crystal stair.

-Langston Hughes

Childhood Reflection

By: Dynasty Finley

I remember when you used to make me do things that I did not want to do.
Making me go to the store and clean up the house—taking me away from my friends.
I couldn't go outside until I finished my homework.
Saying stuff like, "You will never get anywhere in life jokin' around."
Schoolin' me on what is right and wrong .
Yet, I was always the spoiled person out of everyone.
Our good times and bad times fade away so fast.
Uniting with you after your five years of death would be a blessing to my heart.
Putting together all of the things you had me do throughout my life made sense.
Acting more like a mature adult just like you.
Taking you as my guide and leading me to be a successful business woman.

You are the special person in my life, and not a person in this world loves me the way that you did.

I LOVE YOU MOM!

My Worst Day (Childhood Memory)

By: Danny M. Dean

There are a lot of thingz in my childhood that I can remember
Especially thingz that happened in December
A lot of them are bad not good
Thatz what happenz when you live in my hood
I can write a lot of songz and poemz about my life
But like I said, they aren't that nice
I really don't like to talk about me
Thatz why I write under DMD
December iz the month of my birthday
Thatz why sometimez I think thatz my worst day
Cuz everytime it comez around
Something happenz that letz me down
Memoriez and now
A lot of my family I can't be around
Cuz they don't ever remember my birthday
Thatz why itz my worst day

Her Life Ends

By: Christopher Crowder

She left me two years ago
Short but Sweet
Always asking about how my day was
Old with wrinkles
But it didn't change her self-esteem
Didn't use wrinkle cream
Never cared about her looks
But I can say different for me
These things I learned from her
It's your life and thoughts
Don't let the clouds hover over your sunshine
Let the light shine
You'll always look fine
But in your casket I still learn from you
R.I.P.—rest in peace
Look over me and guide me
With the tombstone over your head
You still make me think about life
At least once or twice
During my lifetime
The suffering you felt is love and strength in my heart
You'll always be by my side
Grandma

Untitled

By: Lakeisha Cochran

My childhood is something that I never understood
Of why it was bad,
I never had a dad
This makes me sad, because I'm the best child he had
You may ask, "Who is he?"
But I ask, "Why did he...
Why did he leave me?"
All alone in a home, with one lonely beautiful mom
But I kept my head up to my best
And sometimes I feel like a bird trying to find a new nest
My best thing to do is keep up with the person who loves me most
And that is the host
of my family
As I grew my mom said she knew I would be like her
One strong woman

Growing Up

By: Christopher Crowder

Running in the plains
Always thought girls were strange
Body full of energy
Always—Positively
Telling my parents the simple things
Never wanted fancy chains or rings
As time beat me to the punch
Always wanted money—a bunch
Growing older
Learning from mistakes
Learning that gangs and
Guns were always fake
Now knowing the rules of life
Makes life easier—
Easier to become an achiever
Knowing God is the number one purpose
Never believed in curses
Or superstitions
Now that I know
Because I finally listened…

Childhood Memories

By: Aquanette Lowe

Memories to remember
Just like in sweet November
A day when my mother gave birth to the # 1 contender
A deep treasure that bought so much pleasure to her eyes
I grew up with a destiny in disguise
Since a little angel I grew to become a Devil
To express what I feel at any level
I wrote what came to mind
As I grew older through time
I started to define
My life as it is in hell
And to be honest I can't rebel
Living in this world that wants me to fail

Life Story

By: Earl Norman

going back in my childhood
is a story I will tell
from the ages 6-12
I was an angel—but also bad as hell

at school I acted as a fool
I ran amuck because I thought it was cool
I did everything from hitting teachers
to letting loose—insect creatures

from taking little girls' charms
to pulling school fire alarms
I got into a lot fights
I did everything that wasn't right

I did everything that was nonsense
for my behavior–
I usually ended up in the principle office
at home—I still roamed
playing with matches to start fires
constantly flipping off of beds to see if I could go higher

I really never listened to my mother
even though she whooped me—I never ran for cover
my father wasn't around
he was too busy taking care of business
on the other part of town

I had a wild behavior
I used curses like a sailor
I'll never regret anything that I did
now that I think about it I was only a kid
back then I lost my grandmother
and my first lover
in my 13th year
I had a new career
selling drugs and shedding tears

what could I do?

I wanted paper at an early age
I was serious about the game, but brothers thought it was a phase

I felt as if I was in between a circle of barbed wired
on one side, I had my mother;
on the other was my play brother,
who was killed in a house fire

when I was 14,
I should have been in Sing-Sing
'Cause I did stupid stuff for no reason
maybe it was because
my brother ran out of my life
in the fall season

I robbed people with a cap gun
having sex with no condom
is how I used to have fun

don't worry I'm clean
but my blood was still thirsty for green

so I went back to hustling on the block
I had money in my pockets but I was still hot
I had drugs and a loaded gun on the spot
addiction made me not want to stop
months later my glorious life was dropped
…by two crooked cops

throughout this time I made a lot of
lil' thugs hated me
cause I was about money and not GD's
*cause I was **real** and they was fake G's*
I'm still alive and some nights I wonder how
I ever survived the stuff I've been through.
I've changed…look at me now

BLACK LIKE ME...

I remember Marvin Gaye, usta sing ta me
He had me feelin' like black was tha thing ta be
And suddenly tha ghetto didn't seem so tuff
I thought we had it rough, we always had enough

-Tupac Shakur

A Long Dream

By: Earl Norman

I wish my young life was a long dream.
My soul not awaking until I see that white beam.
An eternity of pain seems shorter than me seeing tomorrow.
Going through hell 24/7, living my young life in hopeless sorrow.
Being with my Grandmother is better than my reality.
Is heaven a place I'm supposed to be?
Being on this cold chilly Earth.
Going through chaos since my birth.
Is this the treatment I should be given?
Obeying the devils wishes is where my life has been driven.
Hoping to make a U-turn, but power and money is what I yearn.
This is what my young life seems and I wish it was nothing more than a
long dream.

Is This **Really** Necessary?

By: Quincita Fleming

Why do people call us out of our names,
when we are not the ones to blame?
Why are we always the ones
to feel so very ashamed?

It's not our fault that we're this way.
It's the way God wanted us to be.
Is it really necessary for people to say,
"You're not the same color as me?"

People should really be ashamed of themselves
For acting this way at times.
But not all people can help it,
which is why we have hate crimes.

So here's a question I have for you—
What do you really think of me?
*Is it **really** necessary*
for you to judge me by what you see?

Ghetto Struggle

By: Christopher Crowder

Life is a struggle for everybody-
But living in the ghetto is the worst.
People think different of me.
Because they don't see,
What I see.
They don't do,
What I do.
Do they believe intelligence—
Can come from the ghetto?
Do they believe success—
Can come from the ghetto?
No they don't.
Who are they?
The prejudiced people.
You know what I'm getting at.
Because living in the ghetto is a struggle.

Hurt

By: Anthony Adams

No woman on earth will ever cry again
At least not when I'm around
And there will never be a case of "he didn't mean to"
*Because **I** will never let **my** black woman down*
Every single woman will always have a man
And every homeless family will always have a plan
Every little boy will always have a big brother
And every crying girl will always have a loving mother
These are the things that most people go through at home everyday
Because of where they live, the kids can't even go out and play
Writing this poem makes the hardest man cry
And reading it, will make the most delicate flower die
Because when I go outside and see a family living in the dirt,
I look at them and only can feel hurt

NIGGA

By: Victoria "Lyric" Holmes

used in the past
as it is today-
the WORD has become
something casual to say.
we use it to describe
our black, beautiful, race
but—
haven't we had
enough disgrace?

the word itself is negative enough alone,
think about being called
boy or nigga
when you are fully grown,
there is no reason why
this word should be used this way-
when we have trillions of other positive words to say.

Stand Strong

By: Christopher Taylor

The world is filled with lots of violence
People walk in fear and silence
But I stand strong
Many talk like nothing happens
But deep inside I know there's sadness
But I stand strong
And I ask myself how can this be?
Is all this turmoil happening only to me?
But I stand strong
How long will we be so corrupt?
We do others wrong for change or a buck
But I stand strong
When will parents stop with the drugs?
They should go home and embrace their children with hugs
But I stand strong
It's true I'm a young black man
Now tell me,
*How strong do **you** other men stand?*

Their Minds and Mine

By: Christopher Crowder

When I walk down a street
I walk with a black hood, that
Sets it's sights toward the sky.
As eyes make contact with me,
they think of me as a provoker.
Probably because of the color I choose to wear.
People with the mind of an evil spirit
wear the color white.
The color of innocence,
they know the contradiction-
they know that it is not true.
That's not all they wear.
They wear masks that have the power
To bring out the innocence in them
When I see them,
They are wearing their nice suits and clothes;
Something most darken people would love to behold
But that's in the past and old,
I'm looking for the future and new
Discovering something better for my generation.
So when I walk down a street,
no longer will I feel the heat of hatred,
because I know what I'm after
And I know what they're after.
Because I'm coal
and they want my life
to be a disaster.

The Difference an "er" Makes

By: Yakie Wilburn

I think the word Nigga is appropriate to use as long as you don't use it to offend someone in a derogatory way. It depends on the way people use it. If you were trying to offend someone you would pronounce every letter and add an "er" at the end. When white people used the word Nigger on our ancestors it was to hurt and degrade them. The only reason it still gets to some people is because of the background history of the word.

In this time and age, instead of letting it hurt us or get to us, we have found a way to adapt and use it in a way that is appropriate. It is very common to hear friends greet each other with: "Whatz'up my Nigga." When we use it today, we drop the "er" and add an "a.". This shows that we are not trying to offend anyone, it's just another part of slang language to us.

Young Black Man

By: Victoria "Lyric" Holmes

A father to a son
A boy to a man,
These are my thoughts of a
Young black man.
Stereotyped
And thought of as a thug,
the doer of evil
And barer of drugs
Growing up fast and
Raised to handle his own,
Mocking music videos
He is often shown,
Looking at rappers with paper in one hand
and a girl on the other.
Looking for a young girl to become
A young mother.
Wanting to do right
but often doing wrong,
Trying to find a place
to really belong,
A brother to sister
a helping hand,
These are my thoughts
of a young black man.

N****What N****Who?

By: Aquannette P. Lowe

You know how our people be
Changing the word Negro
Into a word that starts with N-i-g-g-
Yeah, you know the word finishes with an "a"
But what I'm sayin' is that you fools gonna pay!

You can't replace the word you use for someone every day
Even if it is used to clarify the love or the hate
Come on now—is this word really our fate?
Or does this word really make you bait
In the fight of all fights
Are you really ready to rumble—in the face of the light?

Can you express yourself without using Ng?
Come on now—don't play me!
I know and I can see-
This word you use to express your mind
is not the way it should be
Yeah, people act like that's the way it is
'Cuz they hear it from people like Mike Love and the Dizz
*So when you say N****, what N****who?*
*I say, N****please!*

I'm an American

By: Katana Smith

I'm an American,
I was born here
I am free here
I'm an American
Not a Nigger 'cause I wasn't born in Niger
Not a Spaniard 'cause I don't bear gold
Not Japanese even though I eat sushi
Not Indian 'cause I wasn't mistaken
But an American

Everyone here is an American
Everyone here should be equal
Everyone should be treated fairly
But it's America

Some are called Niggers
Who still uses this to this day?
Brainwashed to destroy and resent each other
Disliked because they were different
Resented because they were better
But still
They are Americans

FROM BEGINNING TO END...

A word is dead
When it is said,
Some say.

I say, it just
Begins to live,
That day.

-Emily Dickenson

Eternity

By: Aquannette Lowe

I give my life to thee
To live in the dark for all eternity

The day I'll see the light
Death'll be leveled with my height

I'll be judge for all the wrong I've done
And honored for all the right

I pray that death'll take me
To a place for all eternity

Whether it's hell on earth
Or heavens in the sky

I'll die with pride
And come back with
Vengeance in my eyes

From Beginning to End

By: Denaar Stemley

In the beginning there was Adam and Eve.
In the beginning you didn't have to be tough.
All your brains gave you enough luck.
In the middle is where the trouble starts.
You gotta be quick,
you gotta be smart.
Never show a weakness
Or you'll get hurt.
In the middle just watch yourself.
Don't do anything bad for your health.
In the end just sit and relax.
You finally got your shot
Sitting on your deathbed.
Because things got hot-
and now you're buried six feet deep.
To you my friend, Rest In Peace!

Living

By: Carey Pulley

People struggle to live today—
You have to watch your back everyday
People try to get you from all sides
All people have to do is to stay calm and speak their minds
They say its better to give than receive
You will have a good life if you believe
Everyday people agree giving
That's the best way—
when you talk about living

Me and Me Only

By: Victoria "Lyric" Holmes

All by myself,
Feeling free as can be,
No worries, no sorrow,
No one to judge me.
I'm not lonely physically
But mentality,
No one is here to understand me,
Maybe this is how it's
Supposed to be—
Me and me only.
No one to make
Me feel like I'm wrong.
No one to make me feel like
I don't belong.
Loving myself and the whole world
But not getting the love back,
That's not a reason to
Make my heart crack,
I'll just stand tall,
Be strong and bold,
A girl ready to be put
Into a woman's mold.

My Purpose

By: Denaar Stemley

What is my purpose here on earth?
Is it to be in a gang?
To claim my turf?
Is it to help children who don't have anything?
Or is it to throw wild parties that are jumping?
Is it to have fun and joke all day?
Is it to get a job or sell drugs to make pay?
Is it to get women pregnant
And then leave them alone?
Or if I get them pregnant-stay home?
Is it to shoot guns and be an out law—
Shooting guns and breaking peoples jaw?
Whatever it is I'm sure it's something nice.
I hope it is to have a job, house, kids and a wife.

The Plan

By: Victoria "Lyric" Holmes

Not ready for the
world yet,
Just trying to get myself set,
Saving for the future
something I hope to see,
Each and everyday
is a miracle to me?
Waking up to see
the morning light,
Wishing the days will go right,
I have plans for my life
to drive a nice car,
To go places really far,
Have a good job
that gives me a nice pay,
To probably have my own
family someday,
Be able to give my children
whatever they need,
So one day they will succeed,
Take care of my mother
because she took care of me,
That seems like that's
how it's supposed to be,
Although I'm not ready
but soon I will,
Until then time
won't stand still.

Untitled

By: Wayne Wicks

I'm lost in a world with people who are fake flossin'
Everywhere I go I see my son-just lost him
Growing up thinkin; he's a pimp, that's gonna cost him
Giving me 100% when he's storin'
Money he ain't got; so ya better start borrowin'
Getting out the hood ain't what lil' man thought
Weed and blunts is what he bought
Comin' home hands smell kind of raw
Back from the zone in my home, naw
Lil' man is now a thug in jail
I bet you his daddy won't pay his bail.

Love....

Baby you don't know, what you do to me.
Between me and you, I feel a chemistry.
Won't let no one come and take your place.
Cause the love you give can't be replaced.
See no one else love me like you do.
That's why I want to spend my life with you.

-Aaliyah

A Beautiful Mystery

By: Paris Finley

When I took one look at you,
I couldn't believe my eyes.
Your looks were astonishing,
It took me by surprise.
I don't know your name,
Or even who you are
But I know you are unique,
Kind of like a shooting star.
Your skin is so smooth
Surely you are too.
For someone that's so nice looking,
There's no one else like you.
I never imagined I would see a boy like you,
Whose body moves with grace
These are the outside appearances,
I bet the inside is the same.
I just wish I knew your name.

Talking

By: Victoria Holmes

The way you talk,
The way you feel,
To express yourself
During an ordeal.
To open your mouth
And speak a word.
To say something no one has ever heard.
To move me without using a thing,
But the words that you may say.
Everything that has breath
Has its own special way.

The Boy

By: Aquannette P. Lowe

The boy came like the wind and tried to win my heart
I told him, "No!" cause I knew it will only fall apart
He kissed me and said, "Please, baby why?
I love you with my whole heart and I would not lie."
But if you loved me so you'll let me be.
My heart is not to be won, but to be free.

The Boy Part 2

He changed my life because of what he felt
Now, if he was to leave, I fear my heart would melt
I love him so, but can not say
So I try to tell him in a different way
I whisper the words I want to say
But the wind blows and steals them away
He looks at me with an expressionless face
Then disappears with the wind without a trace.

I am Coming Home

By: Wayne Wicks

I hate to leave you all alone
And have to use the telephone
You cut me to the bone
But you know I am coming home

I've been away for such a long time
And you know you were always on my mind
Sometimes I can't stop crying
But all I can do I keep on trying

I have just one more thing to say
I love you more and more each and everyday
And when I get home, I'm there to stay
With you forever is what I pray.

Lost Love

By: Victoria "Lyric" Holmes

I thought love was forever
the words are: 'til death to us part,
Even though you're not here
you're still in my heart,
Looking at your picture
a teardrop falls from my eyes,
You're not here to wipe it away
and tell me not to cry.
The thought of you
puts a smile on my face,
And all the thoughts of anger and hatred
fades away and erases.
I saw the picture of you and me
so I began to weep,
I woke up this morning
to find out I cried myself to sleep.

From Around the Way

By: Quincita Fleming

I'm not gonna start off with his name cuz if you see him you might just run into his game he's got it real good and it's never the same his words are always flying high like be careful when he spin it cuz you might just get caught up in it and then you ain't gonna want him to quit it it's strange how his words always change never stay the same but this is true the boy is a playa and he'll play you too you never know when he'll appear wearing his gear in his eyes you're only a smear another girl who he'd like to give a whirl—flip your curls he'd say we can go together undercover but only wants to get you under covers not be your lover cuz better believe he's gonna drop you for another—in trouble he'll make you scream get help on the double moan and groan the boy acts like he's grown minding his own until another girl comes along singing a song never go wrong you hear what I say this boy does this everyday and only stay just a few feet around the way.

Remember

By: Jackie Colon

Remember me, when you're all alone and have no one
To care for you.
Remember me, when you're feeling down and no one's
Around.
Remember me as the fool who fell into your traps.
Remember my smile,
Remember my touch,
Remember the girl that loves you so much!
Remember the times,
Remember the places,
Remember the joys and our smiling faces.
Remember the love that fills our hearts,
Close together or miles apart we'll always be
Heart-to-heart!

You Should've Listened

By: DMD

Me and you been friendz 4 a long time
Now you messin wit a nigga wit an ill mind
You tried 2 hide yo bruisez
And I acted like I didn't see 'em
But when he gave you that black eye, I wanted 2 kill'em
You tried 2 hide it by puttin yo hair over yo eyez
And when you looked me in the face I could see that you wanted 2 cry
At that moment I wanted 2 die
Cause when we was shortyz I told you I was gonna protect you
Thru whatever
Damn, I gotta pull myself 2gether
I saw that nigga around the way
And did what I did
Now you're all up in my face
That had me tripped
You told me 2 leave you alone
I didn't listen
I told you 2 leave him alone
You didn't listen
Next day I saw ya'll kissin
A few weekz later you're in the hospital
And that nigga missin
Damn,
Why didn't you listen?

When I told him I loved him

By: Krystal Montgomery

When I told him I loved him, he said it back.
But love is obviously what he lacks.
But I didn't know
That what he said was just for show.
He looked me in my eyes,
And told me lies.
I couldn't let him go—
Because I loved him so.
Deep in my heart, I knew
That he wasn't true.
When he said it,
I had a fit.
His friends laughed and joked—
When I found out, I choked
I asked him the deal
He said it wasn't real
He said, "Love isn't my game,
And your love, I don't claim!"
I was sad.
Then mad.
I set his car on fire
Took his money, then retired
Now he's broke,
And now it's my time to laugh and joke

What Is Love?

By: Quincita Fleming

*What exactly **is** love?*
I bet if I asked you, you wouldn't know.
Love is when you would do anything for them-
Sometimes just to please them.
Love is when you can work out your many differences,
Come to compromises,
And never leave their side.
*You would **die** for the person you love.*
Would you?
*And I thought you knew what **love** was.*

Your Presence

By: Christopher Crowder

Your presence equals the sun
Your beauty surrounds me with protection
Your smooth, brown hair
The skin on your body
Light as the moon
Always around me
Never in stone
Your lips like silk
Your love's like cow's milk
Your body,
my words
Cannot express
All I know is when I'm down
You give me a lift
My moon, when I'm in the dark
You're there for me when near or apart

Deep inside...
(911)

Do not go gentle into that good night,
Old age should burn and rave at close of day;
Rage, rage against the dying of the light.

-Dylan Thomas

Til Nothingz Left

By: Danny Dean

My rhymes are like stories—
Poetry in motion
When I got this pen in my hand
Itz utter devotion
When I rhyme it comes from pure emotion:
Anger and violence—
Then a complete silence
D startz riotz
I'm like the calm b4 the storm
Then I transform in2 somethin so destructive
You wish you wasn't born
I keep everything mental
Cause I luv 2 make you think.
When you think you sink;
And that keepz me at peace
But never at ease
When I flow I'm like a con artist
Manipulating MC'z
So like hard timez
I spit hard rhymez
That will confuse yo mind
Till there iz nothing left

Freedom Land, USA

By: Victoria "Lyric" Holmes

Why is the world
so very blind?
Suddenly, everyone cares
about all mankind.
They didn't care about racism
In their own land of the free,
When young black men were
Beaten, then hung from a tree,
They didn't see the fiery crosses
In the front yard of their "American Land"
They didn't have their freedom marches stopped
With their people killed where they stood..

But I understand the world deserves
To mourn at this time,
I mean thousands of people died
Without committing a crime,
Maybe September 11, will open everyone's eyes
To actually see
Such things like why have organizations
That hate an African American Family?
What does it matter what God I pray to?
Did my God do anything to you?
Maybe now people will try to understand,
This is the United States of America
The Famous Freedom Land.

The Crime

By: Aquannette P. Lowe

I try so hard to commit the perfect murder
I strive to complete the crime
but it ends up incomplete

Something tells me not to don't do it
That's what they want me to do, to give in, to fail,
to say they were better than me.

But it hurts so much to live on and on in hell
I see the light but cannot enter
I'm nothing more than a child cursed by the devil

The rage inside me is trying to escape
Waiting for that date
When all hell will break
Then the devil's child shall escape
For the child of darkness shall never forgive
all those in her path shall not live

The Dog

By: Danny Dean

I stay red cause I'm bloody
Can't no other dog touch me
Wonder why D act so thugy?
Don't think I'm lucky
I stay dirty
You think that what you do gonna hurt me
Nothing that you can do or say is gonna hurt me
Casualty of war
Got you momma screamin', "Lord have mercy!"
I'm back—
The dog.
I attack wit a vengeance
Got ya'll wonderin when DMD gonna end this?
I will never stop
Even after I'm dropped;
Stories from the grave
Comin' at you nonstop
I'm 2 hot right now
Immortalized like Pac
Thug life 4ever
Iz the world ready for me
Naw

Untitled

By: Jacqueline Colon

As many of the poems I have written
Talk about wanting to die,
To be with all of the people I know,
That I hold dearly, in heaven.
I don't want that anymore
This crisis made me realize that
I don't want to die
I want to live and die later of natural causes
Not because of a mentally diseased, overweight idiot says
IDIOT TERRORISTS
I am only 15 years and 8 months old.
I want, let me rephrase that
I AM going to accomplish ALL of my dreams
I will not give into this religious
Hatred that is going on around the world
It does not make sense to fight over
Your religion or race, because either way you look
At it we are praying to only one God
Who cares what his name is whether it be Allah, God or Yahweh.
Who cares what the "story book" is called?
Bible, Koran, or Torah.
I do not wish death upon anyone
An to tell you the truth, without sounding like an airhead,
I honestly, whole heartedly, and truly want
World Peace. If you really think about it, when
Everyone is at peace, no one is dying.
Very plain, very simple

Untitled

By: June Petty

As I laid in my bed, wishing that it wasn't true
To see the thousands of bodies laying dead
In the Twin Towers
The pain those families are having to face
I find myself terrified.
Not terrified for me—
for the Mothers of mothers,
the Fathers of fathers,
the kids without mothers or fathers now.
I just can't place myself in the place of those
who are looking for their loved ones.
And I just find myself just lying there stunned.

This is why

Look for the words between the lines
Do they fly like birds?
Are they able to fly?
The words that I write
Express my feelings to the world
Because I'm not very good at using my mouth
I say things that I don't mean to say
That's why I use words express my ways
My mouth is a dangerous weapon
That's why I can't use it very much
Poems are my way of life
and expression
I write poems
because I have learned my lesson

By: Christopher Crowder

0-595-21571-8